KITCHEN TO CAREER

# PASTRY WORKSHOP

## Mastering Buttery Crusts & Doughs

Megan Borgert-Spaniol

Abdo & Daughters
MIDDLE GRADE NONFICTION
An imprint of Abdo Publishing
abdobooks.com

ABDOBOOKS.COM

Published by Abdo Publishing, a division of ABDO, PO Box 398166, Minneapolis, Minnesota 55439. Copyright © 2024 by Abdo Consulting Group, Inc. International copyrights reserved in all countries. No part of this book may be reproduced in any form without written permission from the publisher. Abdo & Daughters™ is a trademark and logo of Abdo Publishing.

Printed in the United States of America, North Mankato, Minnesota
052023
092023

Design: Aruna Rangarajan and Emily O'Malley, Mighty Media, Inc.
Production: Mighty Media, Inc.
Editor: Ruthie Van Oosbree
Recipes: Megan Borgert-Spaniol
Cover Photographs: Mighty Media, Inc.; Shutterstock Images
Interior Photographs: INTERFOTO/Alamy Photo, p. 6 (top left); iStockphoto, pp. 4, 5 (bottom), 18 (bottom right), 19 (left), 22, 26, 29 (bottom), 60; Mighty Media, Inc., pp. 21 (all), 23 (bottom right, middle right), 24 (bottom three), 25 (bottom), 30 (pie and plate), 32 (all), 33 (all), 34–35, 36 (tart), 38 (all), 39 (all), 40–41, 42 (turnover and plate), 44 (all), 45 (all), 46–47, 48 (éclairs), 50 (all), 51 (all), 52–53; Shutterstock Images, pp. 3, 5 (top), 6 (bottom, top right), 8, 9, 10, 11 (all), 12 (all), 13 (all), 14, 15 (all), 16 (all), 17 (all), 18 (top, bottom left), 19 (right), 20 (all), 23 (top, left, middle second from right, middle second from top), 24 (top), 25, 27 (all), 28, 29 (top), 30 (background), 36 (background), 42 (background), 48 (background), 54 (all), 55, 56, 57, 58 (all), 59, 61 (all); Wikimedia Commons, p. 7
Design Elements: Shutterstock Images

The following manufacturers/names appearing in this book are trademarks: Artist's Loft™, KitchenAid®, Nordic Ware™, Nutella®, and Wilton®

Library of Congress Control Number: 2022948839

## PUBLISHER'S CATALOGING-IN-PUBLICATION DATA

Names: Borgert-Spaniol, Megan, author.
Title: Pastry workshop: mastering buttery crusts & doughs / by Megan Borgert-Spaniol
Other title: mastering buttery crusts & doughs
Description: Minneapolis, Minnesota : Abdo Publishing, 2024 | Series: Kitchen to career | Includes online resources and index.
Identifiers: ISBN 9781098291426 (lib. bdg.) | ISBN 9781098277888 (ebook)
Subjects: LCSH: Food--Juvenile literature. | Cooking--Juvenile literature. | Baking--Juvenile literature. | Pastry--Juvenile literature. | Dough--Juvenile literature. | Pies--Juvenile literature. | Desserts--Juvenile literature. | Occupations--Juvenile literature.
Classification: DDC 641.865--dc23

# CONTENTS

Making a Career in the Kitchen .............. 5
The Basics ....................................... 7
Getting Started .................................. 11

- ◆ **Apple Pie** .......................... 31
- ◆ **Chocolate Tart** ................... 37
- ◆ **Fruit Turnovers** .................. 43
- ◆ **Chocolate Éclairs** ............. 49

Presentation & Beyond ......................... 54
Careers in the Kitchen ......................... 57
Glossary ......................................... 62
Online Resources ................................ 63
Index ............................................. 64

# MAKING A CAREER IN THE KITCHEN

Are you fascinated by the way butter makes dough rich and flaky? Do you love experimenting with recipes and making tweaks to improve them? Can you see yourself whipping up buttery crusts and delicious fillings for others to enjoy? If your answer to these questions is yes, you might be suited to a career as a pastry chef.

Becoming a pastry chef takes a lot of training and hard work. It takes dedication to craft, quality, and safety. But if you have a passion for pastries, you may find that the dedication comes naturally and the hard work is worthwhile.

In this book, you'll learn about the history of pastries and how pastry making has changed over time. You'll become familiar with basic ingredients, tools, and techniques used to bake pastries. You'll practice using these ingredients, tools, and techniques in a few basic recipes. Then, you'll try your hand at following your own tastes and inspirations to modify recipes. Finally, you'll learn a bit about how you might take your passion for baking pastries from the kitchen into a career.

In Medieval Europe, small, savory pies were a common street food.

Baklava is a dessert made with phyllo dough, nuts, and honey syrup. Early versions of baklava may date back to 800 BCE.

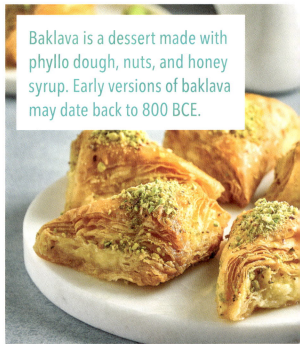

Croissants are made similarly to puff pastry. They are a popular breakfast food in France.

THE BASICS

# INTRODUCTION TO PASTRY

The term *pastry* is often used broadly to describe an array of baked goods. In this book, *pastry* refers to doughs made with the core ingredients of flour, water, and fat. Pastry is distinct from bread for having a higher proportion of fat. The dough is rolled out into thin sheets or piped from a pastry bag.

Pastry dough is used in both sweet and savory recipes. It is featured in pies, tarts, croissants, baklava, and much more. There are five main types of pastry:

**FLAKY PASTRY** is made with pieces of fat that create layers of dough when they melt in the oven.

**SHORTCRUST PASTRY** is made with a well-mixed dough that creates a sturdy, crumbly pastry, similar to a shortbread cookie.

**PUFF PASTRY** is made by laminating dough, or repeatedly folding fat into the dough, creating a flaky texture. In the process, fat and air are trapped between layers of dough. This causes the layers to puff up during baking.

**CHOUX PASTRY** dough has a higher water content than other pastry doughs. The water evaporates to create steam, which puffs up the pastry. After baking, choux pastry is hollow inside with a crisp outer shell.

**PHYLLO PASTRY** is made by stacking very thin sheets of dough, which bake up into delicate layers.

People around the world have made pastries for thousands of years. Ancient Egyptians, Greeks, and Romans all used a phyllo-type dough to make cakes, tarts, and other pastries. The Romans created a basic pastry dough to cover meat and keep it moist while it cooked. After cooking, the pastry was discarded, not eaten.

An ancient Egyptian bakery

Electric ovens **became popular in the 1920s and 1930s.** By 2018, most **ovens in the United States were electric.**

Over the years, pastry making became distinct from bread baking in western Europe. During the Crusades, from 1095 to 1291, sugar and early puff pastry were brought to Europe from Persia. These helped further distinguish pastry.

In the 1600s, pastry making became more popular. People used pastry to make more detailed, decorative foods. New ingredients, technologies, and techniques led to new types of pastries. A French man named Marie-Antoine Carême is particularly known for his many pastry innovations, including his contribution to puff pastry techniques. Thanks in part to his work, French pastry desserts became associated with fine dining. Many modern pastry recipes have their origins in French pâtisserie, or pastry. In France, the term refers to a variety of delicate, flaky, and beautifully decorated baked goods.

During the 1700s and 1800s, industrialization brought greater access to baking technologies like ovens, so more people could bake at home. Meanwhile, globalization allowed for the spread of knowledge. With increased access to ingredients, recipes, and techniques from around the world, pastry makers could master all kinds of different pastries.

Today, pastries are made worldwide by both home bakers and trained pastry chefs. In the following pages, you'll learn about common ingredients, tools, and techniques in pastry making. Then you'll be ready to get baking!

Marie-Antoine Carême invented a dessert called croquembouche. It is a cone of choux pastry puffs held together with wisps of caramel.

GETTING STARTED

# INGREDIENTS

Get familiar with some of the ingredients you'll see in this book's recipes.

### BUTTER

Butter is a fat typically made from cow's milk. For baking, use unsalted butter unless a recipe specifically calls for salted butter. Many pastry doughs require cold butter, which helps create flaky layers. Butter also adds rich flavor and smooth texture to fillings.

### CINNAMON

Cinnamon is a spice made from a type of tree bark. It adds a warm, slightly sweet flavor to pastries and other baked goods. Cinnamon is especially popular in pastries that feature apples, peaches, pumpkin, and other fruits.

### CORNSTARCH

Cornstarch is a fine powder made from corn. It is used to thicken custards and other sauces made for pastries, including pastry cream. You can use all-purpose flour in place of cornstarch, but you'll need twice as much flour as you would cornstarch.

### EGGS

Eggs help bind and thicken pastry doughs and fillings. They also act as leaveners because their proteins trap air bubbles. Finally, the fats in eggs bring rich flavor and color to pastries.

### FLOUR

The recipes in this book call for all-purpose flour. This is a blend of wheat flours that can be used to bake a variety of foods, from crusty breads to fluffy cakes. However, some pastry recipes call for bread flour, which has a higher protein content than all-purpose flour. The extra protein allows for strong layers in pastry dough. Flour is also used to thicken fruit fillings.

### FRUIT JAM OR PRESERVES

Fruit fillings are popular in pastries such as tarts and turnovers. Both jam and preserves can be used for pastry fillings. These fruit spreads are both made of fruit cooked with sugar, but preserves contain more chunks of fruit than jam does.

### MILK & HEAVY CREAM

The fat in milk and cream help make pastry fillings and icings smooth. Milk is also used to tenderize and add a golden color to some pastry doughs, such as choux. If a recipe does not call for a specific type of milk, use whole or 2 percent milk.

### SALT

Salt is a mineral that adds its own flavor and enhances other flavors. If a recipe does not call for a specific type of salt, regular table salt will do. Some recipes call for kosher salt, which is made of coarser grains than table salt. A sprinkle of flaky sea salt adds bursts of flavor and crunch to some pastries, especially those featuring chocolate or caramel.

### SEMISWEET CHOCOLATE

Semisweet chocolate has about 40 to 60 percent cocoa. This produces a nice balance of sweetness and bitterness. You can melt down semisweet bars, wafers, or chips for use in pastry fillings and icings.

### SUGAR

Sugar is used to sweeten pastry doughs and fillings. Sometimes it is sprinkled on top of the doughs for added texture and sweetness. There are several varieties of sugar, but recipes that call for simply "sugar" are referring to granulated sugar, or white sugar.

### VANILLA EXTRACT

Pure vanilla extract is made by soaking vanilla beans in an alcohol solution. This pulls out the flavors of the vanilla beans and concentrates them in liquid form. Vanilla extract adds a subtle caramel flavor to pastry fillings and icings.

# KITCHEN TOOLS

Get familiar with some of the supplies you'll see in this book's recipes.

### BAKING SHEET

A baking sheet is a pan with a shallow outer rim around all four sides or no rim at all. Use a rimmed sheet for filled pastries that might leak while baking, such as fruit turnovers.

### COOLING RACK

A cooling rack allows air to circulate around a hot pan or dish, helping it cool faster than it would on a solid surface.

### DOUGH SCRAPER

A dough scraper is a rectangular piece of steel with a handle. Its dull blade end is used for dividing doughs. Some dough scrapers are made of plastic instead of metal. They are strong enough to cut through dough but also flexible enough to scrape dough out of bowls and off mixing equipment.

### ELECTRIC MIXER

Both stand mixers and handheld mixers use electricity to blend and whip pastry fillings, such as pastry cream or whipped cream. An electric mixer also comes in handy when whipping eggs into choux dough.

### PARCHMENT PAPER

Parchment paper is a heat-resistant nonstick paper that helps prevent pastries from burning or sticking to baking sheets. Parchment paper is good for only one or two uses. If you want to avoid paper waste, a silicone baking mat does the job of parchment paper but is washable and reusable.

### PASTRY BRUSH

A pastry brush is a soft-bristled brush used to spread egg wash over dough. If you don't have a pastry brush, you can do the same job with an unused paintbrush, the back of a spoon, or even your fingers.

### PASTRY BAG & TIP

A pastry bag or piping bag is a cone-shaped bag that holds pastry doughs, pastry fillings, frostings, and icings that must be piped. The bag is filled through its larger open end. The filling is then squeezed out of the smaller open end, which is often fitted with a metal tip that shapes the piped filling. If you do not have a pastry bag and tip, scoop your dough or filling into a large plastic bag and cut an opening in one of the bag's bottom corners.

### PIE DISH

A pie dish or pie plate is a round, deep pan with slanted sides. Pie dishes come in a variety of diameters and depths. A standard dish that works for most recipes has a diameter of 8½ to 10 inches (21.6 to 25.4 cm) and a depth of 1½ to 2 inches (3.8 to 5.1 cm).

### PIE WEIGHTS

Pie weights are metal or ceramic balls used to weigh down tarts and pies that need to bake without a filling. The weights keep the pastry from puffing up or otherwise losing its shape while it bakes. You can use dried beans, rice, or popcorn kernels in place of metal or ceramic pie weights.

### PLASTIC WRAP

Plastic wrap, or cling wrap, is a thin plastic film used to cover foods. Bakers wrap pastry doughs and cover pastry creams in plastic wrap before chilling them in the refrigerator. The wrap creates an airtight seal that prevents the dough or cream from drying out. To avoid plastic waste, some bakers use reusable plastic bags or beeswax wrap instead.

### ROLLING PIN

A rolling pin is a long, cylindrical tool used to evenly flatten doughs. Don't have a rolling pin? Try using a reusable water bottle or thermos that has an even diameter.

### TART PAN

A tart pan is a shallow pan with vertical sides that are often fluted. Many tart pans have removable bottoms. This makes it easy to remove the crust from the pan after baking.

### WHISK

A whisk is used to thoroughly blend fine ingredients, such as flour, sugar, and salt. A whisk is also good for incorporating air into an ingredient, such as eggs or cream. For mixing doughs, use a stronger tool, like a wooden spoon or rubber spatula.

# TERMS & TECHNIQUES

Get familiar with some of the terms and techniques you'll see in this book's recipes.

## CHILLING DOUGH

Most pastry recipes call for chilling the dough at least once. If you're feeling rushed, you may be tempted to skip the chill. Don't! This crucial step allows the fat in the dough to firm up after being handled. Chilling also allows the gluten in the dough to relax, making the dough easier to roll out and shape.

## EGG WASH

An egg wash is a whisked egg, sometimes combined with milk or water, that is brushed over dough before baking. The wash gives the final product a nice golden color.

## PIPING

Pastry recipes that involve soft dough, creamy fillings, or decorative frostings require piping, or squeezing a mixture from a bag onto a surface. Sometimes special tips or nozzles are used to create distinct shapes. Piping techniques vary depending on the mixture you are piping, the nozzle you are using, and the shape you are making. Pipe a few practice shapes on a plate or piece of parchment paper to get a feel for the pressure and angle to use when piping.

## FLOURING THE WORK SURFACE

Pastry recipes often call for doughs to be rolled out on a floured surface. Start with a light, even sprinkle of flour over a clean, dry surface. If the dough starts to stick, sprinkle a little more flour onto the surface.

### PREHEATING THE OVEN

Pastries and most other baked goods rely on an initial blast of heat to kick-start their rise. That's why it's important to preheat your oven, or let it fully heat to the specified temperature, before you start baking.

### SEPARATING EGG YOLKS FROM WHITES

An egg consists of the yellow yolk and the white. The yolk contains fat that brings a rich flavor and smooth texture to pastry doughs or fillings. The white contains protein that gives structure to baked goods. Some pastry recipes call for just egg yolks. To separate the yolk from the white, crack the egg over a container where you will store the white. Gently pass the yolk back and forth between the shell halves until all of the white has slipped off the yolk and into the container. Then place the yolk in a different container. Save the whites for a breakfast omelet!

### SIMMERING VERSUS BOILING

Some pastry doughs and fillings require cooking on the stove. If a recipe says to heat a liquid to a simmer, look for small bubbles that rise to the liquid's surface, causing gentle movement. If a recipe calls for boiling the liquid, look for many large bubbles rising at once, constantly disrupting the liquid's surface.

### TOSSING TOGETHER

Tossing refers to mixing two ingredients lightly until one is well-coated with the other. For example, cold butter is tossed in flour, apples are tossed in cinnamon, and tomatoes are tossed in oil. Tossing requires more of an upward motion than stirring and is often done with clean hands instead of spoons or spatulas.

### VENTING

Filled pastries such as pies and turnovers require vents, or slits, cut into the dough. This allows steam to escape as the pie bakes. Pastries made with choux dough, such as éclairs and cream puffs, also benefit from venting. In this case, the vent is cut after the pastry comes out of the oven. This prevents the inside of the pastry from getting soggy from unreleased steam.

## KITCHEN PREP TIPS

> Have all your supplies out and ready before you begin. Gather all your ingredients on a tray or rimmed baking sheet. Then it's easy to slide everything out of the way if you need to make space.

> Wear an apron to protect your clothing. It will also serve as a hand towel.

# SHORTCRUST & FLAKY PASTRY BASICS

Shortcrust and flaky pastry doughs are used to make tarts and pies. Here are a few basic techniques to keep in mind as you work with these doughs.

Overworking pie and tart dough makes the dough tough. It can also cause butter to melt into the flour. You want to preserve the pockets of cold butter—those are what create flaky layers in the crust. Use ice-cold water in your dough, and stop working the dough as soon as it comes together.

After the dough disk chills, lightly flour the work surface and rolling pin. Place the dough disk on the surface and roll it out. Every few rolls, rotate the disk a quarter turn to help keep its circular shape and ensure it isn't sticking to the surface. If the dough starts to stick to the surface, lift the dough with a dough scraper and sprinkle more flour underneath. Keep the rolling pin floured too so the dough doesn't stick to it.

There are several methods of transferring pie and tart dough from the work surface to the pan. One method is to roll the dough around the rolling pin and then unroll it into the pan. Another method is to fold the dough in half or quarters and then unfold it into the pan.

To make an egg wash, whisk an egg in a small bowl. Then use a pastry brush to lightly cover your pastry dough with the wash. Without an egg wash, many pastries will appear pale. An exception is choux pastry, which contains several eggs, giving it a natural golden color.

# CHOUX PASTRY BASICS

Choux pastry dough is used to make éclairs, cream puffs, and similar light, airy pastries. This thick, sticky dough is piped instead of rolled out. Here are a few basic techniques to keep in mind as you work with choux dough.

Place the pastry bag in a tall glass and fold the bag's edges around the rim of the glass. This frees up both your hands to fill the bag with dough or cream.

If you are piping éclairs, draw straight lines in pencil on the back of the parchment paper to provide a template so your éclairs are straight and even.

Pipe a dot of choux dough onto each corner of the pan before placing parchment paper on top. This secures the paper to the pan while you pipe your éclairs or cream puffs.

Pipe cream puffs at a 90-degree angle, and pipe éclairs at a 45-degree angle. Use even pressure when piping éclairs to keep a consistent thickness.

Cutting a slit into baked choux creates a vent for steam to escape, preventing soggy interiors. To help the choux pastries dry out, cut the vents and put the pastries back into the warm oven with the door open for five minutes.

# FOOD SAFETY TIPS

> Make sure your prep surface is clean and dry. Wash your hands with soap and water before and after you handle ingredients.
> Don't eat doughs containing uncooked flour or eggs.
> Place any leftover ingredients into containers with lids. Use tape and markers to label the container with the ingredient and the date. Then keep it somewhere you will easily see it so you don't forget about it.

25

# CREATING IN THE KITCHEN

Recipes are great for learning how to bake. But as you get comfortable following recipes, you might start imagining ways to improve them.

Maybe you want to incorporate caramel into your apple pie. Or maybe you decide to sweeten your turnover filling with some honey or maple syrup.

This book includes four formal pastry recipes meant to help you practice working with different ingredients and techniques. Following each formal recipe is an informal companion. These companion recipes are less structured and provide fewer details. This leaves room for you, the baker, to follow your own tastes and preferences. If an informal recipe doesn't suit your taste, check out the accompanying "Experiment!" sidebar for additional ideas. With some thought and creativity, you can make any recipe your own way.

## CONVERSION CHART

| Standard | Metric |
| --- | --- |
| ¼ teaspoon | 1.25 mL |
| ½ teaspoon | 2.5 mL |
| 1 teaspoon | 5 mL |
| 1 tablespoon | 15 mL |
| ¼ cup | 60 mL |
| ⅓ cup | 80 mL |
| ½ cup | 125 mL |
| ⅔ cup | 160 mL |
| ¾ cup | 175 mL |
| 1 cup | 240 mL |
| 325°F | 160°C |
| 350°F | 180°C |
| 375°F | 190°C |
| 400°F | 200°C |
| 425°F | 220°C |

# RULES TO REMEMBER

As you start putting your own twist on recipes, keep these guiding principles in mind.

**Master the basics first.** Start out following recipes exactly as they are written. You'll better understand how ingredients combine and behave, and this knowledge will inform your decisions as you go off-book.

**Every baker has their own methods.** You might see another baker making pie dough with a pastry blender. Or a pastry chef may pipe choux pastry differently than you learned. This doesn't mean you have to use the same pastry blender or pipe the same way. If you can, ask a baker why their methods work for them. Test the methods yourself and decide what works best for you!

**Experiments don't always go to plan.** Don't worry if your puff pastry didn't rise properly or your pie crust burned a bit around the edges. If your results are still edible, don't let them go to waste! Instead, think of how you can repurpose them. If your shortcrust is crumbling, use the broken bits as a topping. If your éclairs are too flat to slice in half, cut pieces to layer in a glass with the pastry cream and chocolate icing.

**Baking is often called a precise science.** But a recipe won't be ruined by an extra egg here or a missed teaspoon of salt there. Bakers are always tweaking and testing their recipes. Enjoy the process and take pride in the results.

## MAKE THIS!

# APPLE PIE

Pies are made with flaky pastry dough. This type of dough requires small bits of cold butter and minimal handling.

## INGREDIENTS

**DOUGH:**
- 2½ cups all-purpose flour
- 1 teaspoon salt
- 1 cup (two sticks) cold unsalted butter
- ¼ cup ice water
- 1 egg (for egg wash)

**FILLING:**
- ½ cup sugar
- 1 tablespoon cinnamon
- 2 tablespoons flour
- ¼ teaspoon salt
- about 5 cups peeled and sliced apples (about 6 medium apples)

## SUPPLIES

- vegetable peeler
- knife and cutting board
- measuring cups and spoons
- whisk
- mixing bowls
- dough scraper (optional)
- plastic wrap
- refrigerator
- rolling pin
- 9-inch (22.9 cm) pie dish
- oven
- mixing spoon
- fork
- pastry brush
- aluminum foil (optional)
- cooling rack

**1** To make the dough, whisk together the flour and salt in a medium bowl. Cut the chilled butter into ½-inch (1.3 cm) cubes and add them to the bowl.

**2**

With your hands, toss the butter cubes in the flour mixture so they are coated. Then use your fingers to smash the butter into the flour mixture, creating a shaggy mixture of thin, flat bits of butter covered in flour. Work quickly so the butter doesn't soften.

**3** Drizzle the ice water into the bowl and use your fingers to incorporate the liquid. Work the mixture into a rough dough ball.

**4**

Transfer the dough to a clean, dry surface. Shape the dough into a ball. Then divide it into two equal portions.

**5** Flatten each portion to a disk about 1 inch (2.5 cm) thick and wrap it in plastic. Chill the wrapped dough disks in the refrigerator for at least one hour.

**6**

To make the filling, mix the sugar, cinnamon, flour, and salt in a small bowl. Place the sliced apples in a large bowl. Add the sugar-cinnamon mix to the bowl of apples and toss everything together until the apple slices are evenly coated.

7  Place one disk of chilled dough on a lightly floured surface. Roll it out into a 12-inch (30.5 cm) circle about 1/8 inch (0.3 cm) thick.

8  Transfer the dough into the pie dish and lightly press it against the bottom and sides.

9  Place the pie dish back in the refrigerator while you roll out the second dough disk the same way you did the first. While you roll out the second disk, preheat the oven to 425°F.

10  Take the pie dish out of the refrigerator and pour in the filling. Place the second dough disk over the filling.

11  Use a fork to seal the top layer of dough to the bottom layer.

12  Brush the top of the pie with an egg wash. Then use a knife to make five or six slits in the top for venting.

13  Bake the pie for 40 to 45 minutes. If the edges of the pie are getting dark, take it out of the oven and place strips of aluminum foil over the edges. Then continue baking. The crust should be golden and the filling should be bubbling.

14  Let the pie cool on a cooling rack for an hour or two before slicing.

MAKE IT YOUR WAY

# CHEESE & TOMATO GALETTE

A galette is like a free-form pie. Its single crust is folded over at the edges to hold a sweet or savory filling.

Prepare the pie dough and let it chill (you only need one dough disk for a galette, so cut the recipe in half or freeze the extra disk for another day). In a bowl, toss together about 2 cups of halved cherry tomatoes, 2 chopped cloves of garlic, and a big pinch of kosher salt. Set the bowl aside.

Roll out the chilled dough like you would to make a pie. Transfer the dough to a baking sheet lined with parchment. Preheat the oven to 400°F.

## EXPERIMENT!

Try other savory fillings for your galette, such as mushrooms, asparagus, or squash. If you'd rather have something sweet, use apples and cinnamon, strawberries and chocolate, or pears and honey.

Sprinkle about ¾ cup of shredded Parmesan, Asiago, or Gouda cheese over the dough, leaving a 1-inch (2.5 cm) border. Drain the tomatoes to get rid of excess liquid. Then spread the tomatoes over the cheese.

Fold the edges of the dough over the tomato filling. Brush the dough with an egg wash. Season the filling with salt and pepper, then bake the galette for about 50 to 60 minutes.

## MAKE THIS!

# CHOCOLATE TART

Tarts are made with shortcrust pastry dough. It's less flaky and more crumbly than pie dough. It also provides a solid base for fillings both sweet and savory!

## INGREDIENTS

DOUGH:
- 1½ cups all-purpose flour
- 3 tablespoons sugar
- ¼ teaspoon salt
- ½ cup (1 stick) cold unsalted butter
- 1 egg yolk separated from white
- 2 tablespoons ice water

FILLING:
- ¾ cup heavy cream
- ¼ cup milk
- 2 tablespoons sugar
- 10 ounces (284 g) semisweet chocolate chips
- 1 teaspoon vanilla
- ¼ teaspoon salt
- 2 tablespoons unsalted butter

## SUPPLIES

- measuring cups and spoons
- whisk
- mixing bowls
- knife and cutting board
- plastic wrap
- refrigerator
- rolling pin
- dough scraper (optional)
- 9½-inch (24.1 cm) tart pan
- oven
- parchment paper
- pie weights
- cooling rack
- saucepan
- stove
- spatula

**1** To make the dough, whisk together the flour, sugar, and salt in a medium bowl.

**2** Cut the cold butter into ½-inch (1.3 cm) cubes and add them to the bowl.

**3** With your hands, toss the butter cubes in the flour mixture so they are coated. Then use your fingers to work the butter into the flour until the butter bits are the size of coarse crumbs. Work quickly so the butter doesn't soften.

In a small bowl, whisk together the egg yolk and ice water. Make a well in the center of the flour mixture and pour the yolk mixture into it.

**5** Use your hands to gently incorporate the flour mixture into the yolk mixture.

Squeeze a handful of the dough. If it crumbles, work in more cold water 1 tablespoon at a time. If the dough holds together, form it into a disk about 1 inch (2.5 cm) thick. Wrap it in plastic and chill it in the refrigerator for at least one hour.

Place the chilled dough on a lightly floured surface. Roll it out into a 12-inch (30.5 cm) circle about ¼ inch (0.6 cm) thick.

**8**

Transfer the dough to the tart pan and lightly press it against the bottom and sides. Carefully run the knife along the rim of the pan to cut off excess dough. Then place the tart pan in the refrigerator to chill while you preheat the oven to 375°F.

**9**

Line the tart dough with parchment and pour in your pie weights. Bake the crust for about 15 minutes.

**10** Remove the weights and parchment and bake the crust for another 10 to 15 minutes, or until the crust is lightly golden. Let the crust cool on a cooling rack while you make the filling.

**11** To make the filling, whisk the heavy cream, milk, and sugar in a saucepan on the stove until the liquid is hot but not bubbling.

**12**

Pour the semisweet chocolate chips into a medium bowl and pour the hot cream over the chocolate. Stir until smooth. Then stir in the vanilla, salt, and butter until the butter is melted and fully blended.

**13** Pour the filling into the cooled tart crust. Let the filling set in the refrigerator for one or two hours before serving.

[ MAKE IT YOUR WAY ]

# LEMON TARTLETS

Divide your tart dough into tartlets and complete them with a simple, tasty filling.

Make and chill the tart dough. Then divide the dough into 2-tablespoon balls. Grease a muffin pan with butter and place a dough ball in each cup. Place parchment paper over each ball and use the bottom of a small cup or glass to flatten the ball into the muffin cup, creating the tartlet crust.

## EXPERIMENT!

Play with other sweet fillings for your tartlets, such as jams, curds, fresh berries, puddings, or caramel. Or fill your crusts with eggs and veggies for mini quiches.

Use an electric mixer to whip together one 14-ounce can sweetened condensed milk and ½ cup lemon juice until the mixture is smooth and thick.

Bake the tartlet crusts at 350°F for about 10 minutes. Take them out and use the cup or glass to gently press the crusts again, helping them keep their shape. Then put them back in the oven for 10 to 15 more minutes.

Pour the lemon filling into the cooled tartlet crusts. If you'd like, top with whipped cream or lemon zest!

MAKE THIS!

# FRUIT TURNOVERS

Turnovers are often made with puff pastry, a flaky pastry made by layering fat and dough. This is a time-consuming process, so many bakers make rough puff pastry. This is similar to pie dough, but a special folding technique creates lots of delicate layers.

## INGREDIENTS

- 2 cups all-purpose flour
- 1 teaspoon sugar, plus more for dusting
- 1 teaspoon salt
- ¾ cup (1½ sticks) cold unsalted butter
- ¼–½ cup ice water
- 1 egg (for egg wash)
- fruit jam or preserves of your choice

## SUPPLIES

- measuring cups and spoons
- whisk
- mixing bowls
- knife and cutting board
- rolling pin
- dough scraper (optional)
- plastic wrap
- refrigerator
- pizza cutter (optional)
- baking sheet
- parchment paper
- pastry brush
- fork
- oven
- cooling rack

**1** Whisk together the flour, sugar, and salt in a medium bowl. Cut the chilled butter into ½-inch (1.3 cm) cubes and add them to the bowl.

**2** Use your hands to toss the butter cubes in the flour so they are coated. Then use your fingers to smash the butter into the flour, creating a shaggy mixture of thin, flat bits of butter. Work quickly so the butter doesn't soften.

**3** Drizzle ¼ cup of the ice water into the bowl and use your fingers to incorporate the liquid. Add more water, 1 tablespoon at a time, until the dough holds together. Form it into a rough ball.

**4**

Roll the dough out into a rectangle that is ½ inch (1.3 cm) thick. Fold the dough into thirds like you would a letter. Then wrap it in plastic and refrigerate for at least one hour.

**5**

On a lightly floured surface, roll the folded dough out into a rectangle that is ½ inch (1.3 cm) thick. Again, fold the dough into thirds like a letter.

**6** Rotate the dough 90 degrees and repeat step 5.

**7** Rotate the dough 90 degrees and repeat step 5 one more time.

**8** Wrap the folded dough in plastic and refrigerate it for at least 30 minutes.

**9**

On a lightly floured surface, roll out the folded dough into a rectangle about ⅛ inch (0.3 cm) thick. Use a pizza cutter or knife to divide the rectangle into 4-inch (10.2 cm) squares. Place the squares on a baking sheet lined with parchment paper.

**10**

Brush an egg wash along the edges of each dough square. Then place 1 tablespoon of fruit jam or preserves onto the center of each square.

**11**

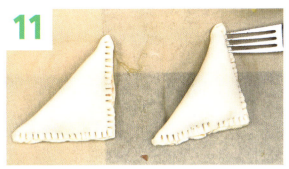

Fold the squares in half diagonally. Use a fork to seal the edges of the dough.

**12** Place the pan of turnovers in the refrigerator for about 30 minutes to chill. Preheat the oven to 400°F.

**13**

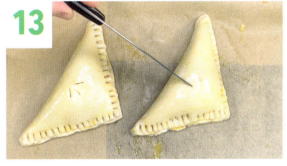

Brush the chilled turnovers with egg wash. Then sprinkle some sugar over them. Use a knife to make three slits in the top of each turnover for venting.

**14** Bake the turnovers for 20 to 25 minutes or until they are golden brown. Let them cool on a cooling rack before serving.

MAKE IT YOUR WAY

# NUTELLA TWISTS

Try forming your puff pastry into long twists!

Prepare puff pastry dough through its final fold and chill (step 8 in the Fruit Turnovers recipe). Then roll it out into a rectangle that is 1/8 inch (0.3 cm) thick and spread a thin layer of Nutella over it.

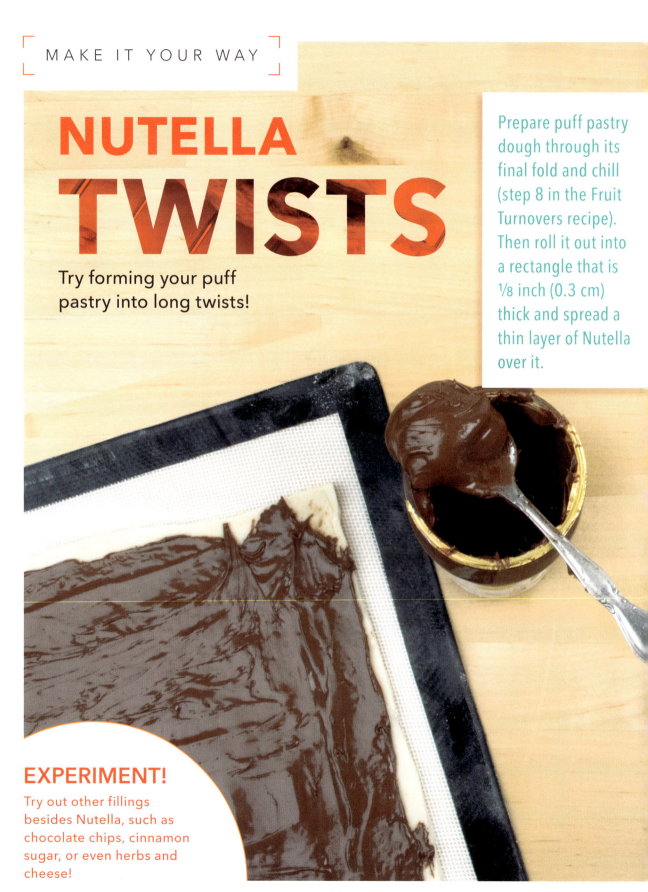

**EXPERIMENT!**
Try out other fillings besides Nutella, such as chocolate chips, cinnamon sugar, or even herbs and cheese!

Fold the dough in half from one short end to the other so the Nutella is between two layers of dough. Use a pizza cutter or knife to cut the dough into strips that are 1 inch (2.5 cm) wide. Twist each strip and place it on a baking sheet lined with parchment.

Brush the twists with an egg wash. Then bake them at 400°F for about 20 minutes or until golden brown.

[ MAKE THIS! ]

# CHOCOLATE ÉCLAIRS

French éclairs feature choux pastry, a thick and sticky dough that comes together on the stove. Steam escapes the dough in the oven, creating a crispy shell and light interior.

## INGREDIENTS

**PASTRY CREAM:**
- 2 cups whole milk
- ½ cup sugar
- ¼ teaspoon salt
- ¼ cup cornstarch
- 4 egg yolks separated from whites
- 2 tablespoons butter
- 1 teaspoon vanilla extract

**DOUGH:**
- ½ cup milk
- ½ cup water
- ½ teaspoon salt
- ½ cup (1 stick) unsalted butter
- 1 cup all-purpose flour
- 4 eggs

**CHOCOLATE ICING:**
- ½ cup semisweet chocolate chips
- ¼ cup heavy cream

## SUPPLIES

- measuring cups and spoons
- whisk
- mixing bowls
- saucepans
- stove
- plastic wrap
- refrigerator
- pastry bag(s) with ⅝-inch (1.6 cm) tip
- wooden spoon
- electric mixer
- oven
- parchment paper
- baking sheet
- water
- cooling rack
- knife
- microwave-safe bowl
- stirring spoon or spatula

**1** To make the pastry cream, whisk the milk, sugar, and salt together in a medium saucepan. Cook the mixture on the stove over medium heat until it comes to a simmer.

**2** While the milk mixture heats, whisk the cornstarch and egg yolks together in a medium bowl until smooth. Once the milk mixture comes to a simmer, whisk ½ cup of it into the bowl with the egg mixture. Whisk in another ½ cup of the milk until smooth.

**3** Pour the milk-egg mixture back into the saucepan and whisk it into the rest of the hot milk. Cook, stirring constantly, until the mixture is thick and bubbling, creating the pastry cream.

**4** Take the pastry cream off the heat and pour it into a medium bowl. Whisk in the butter and vanilla extract until smooth.

**5** Place a piece of plastic wrap over the bowl so it is touching the top of the cream. Cool it in the refrigerator for at least two hours, then transfer it to a pastry bag.

**6** To make the choux dough, combine the milk, water, salt, and butter in a medium saucepan. Heat the mixture over medium-high heat until it comes to a boil.

**7** Carefully pour in the flour and stir with a wooden spoon for about two minutes, until a thick dough forms. Transfer the dough to a large mixing bowl and let it cool for about five minutes.

**8**

Use an electric mixer to beat the eggs into the dough one at a time. After adding the last egg, continue beating until the dough is smooth and glossy.

**9**

Preheat the oven to 425°F. Transfer the dough to the pastry bag. Pipe 3-inch (7.6 cm) éclairs on a parchment-lined baking sheet. Smooth out pointed tips by dipping a finger in water and gently pressing on the dough.

**10** Bake the éclairs for 15 minutes. Then reduce the oven temperature to 350°F and continue baking for 20 to 25 more minutes. They should be dry and golden brown.

**11** Place the éclairs on a cooling rack. Use a sharp knife to cut a vent in the top of each éclair for steam to escape. When they are cool enough to handle, slice them in half the long way to create top and bottom pieces. Let the slices cool completely.

**12** To make the chocolate icing, pour the chocolate chips and heavy cream into a microwave-safe bowl. Heat the mixture in the microwave for 30 seconds at a time, stirring after each round, until smooth.

**13**

Dip the top slices of the choux pastry into the chocolate icing and let the icing set. Assemble the éclairs by piping pastry cream over the bottom slices of the choux pastry and placing the iced slices on top.

MAKE IT YOUR WAY

# CREAM PUFFS

Try baking your choux pastry into round puffs and filling them with sweetened whipped cream!

Instead of piping long éclairs, pipe the choux dough into round puffs about 1½ inches (3.8 cm) in diameter and ½ inch (1.3 cm) tall.

## EXPERIMENT!

You can also cut your cream puffs into top and bottom halves, piping the cream in between. Or replace the whipped cream with ice cream and drizzle hot fudge over the top!

Bake the puffs at the same temperatures and times as you would the éclairs. Let them cool fully.

Whip together 1 cup heavy cream, 2 tablespoons sugar, and ½ teaspoon vanilla extract until fluffy. Poke a hole in the bottom of each cooled puff and pipe in the whipped cream.

# PRESENTATION & BEYOND

Your pastry is baked, but you're not done yet! It's time to think about how to display and serve your creation. Just as important is how you preserve any leftovers.

Present whole pies and let people cut their own slices. Serve the pie with ice cream, whipped cream, or other topping options on the side so people can dress up their slices as much or as little as they'd like.

Top a tart with sea salt, toasted nuts, caramel, or fruit to add color, texture, and artistic flair to your presentation.

For added **sweetness** and texture, **drizzle icing** made of milk and **powdered sugar** over fruit turnovers. Serve them with a side of the **fruit filling!**

If you can, serve éclairs and cream puffs within a few hours of assembling. Arrange them on napkins or cupcake liners for mess-free eating!

## STORING PASTRIES

Fruit-filled pastries can sit at room temperature for one or two days. Cream-filled pastries should be stored in the refrigerator. If you need to keep any pastry for more than a couple days, store it in the freezer, which is cold enough to preserve the pastry's freshness. Cover pies and tarts with plastic wrap and aluminum foil to create an airtight seal before freezing. Wrap handheld pastries such as turnovers individually and then freeze them in a sealed bag or container.

## SPECIAL CONSIDERATIONS

- If you can, only fill choux pastries you will eat within a day. Store leftover choux pastry in the refrigerator or freezer and leftover filling and icing in the refrigerator.

- If you've already iced and filled your choux, freeze the pastries in a single layer on a baking sheet until the icing and filling are set. Then the pastries can be stacked in a bag or container and put back in the freezer.

CAREERS IN THE KITCHEN

# BECOMING A PASTRY CHEF

As you gain more knowledge and experience making pastries, you might decide to turn your hobby into a living. There are many ways to pursue a career in pastry arts!

### FORMAL SCHOOLING
Culinary and technical schools offer pastry programs that can last six months to a few years. These programs offer instruction in pastries and other baked goods. They also prepare students for work in professional kitchens.

### APPRENTICESHIP
Professional kitchens offer hands-on experience through apprenticeships and internships. These positions are often part-time and unpaid.

### ON-THE-JOB TRAINING
Some establishments hire employees with no formal training. New pastry cooks learn from experienced coworkers. Often, a new cook's wages increase as they gain more experience.

### SELF-TEACHING
Many professional pastry chefs learned what they know by reading cookbooks, watching others, and practicing in their own kitchens.

# PASTRY CHEFS AT WORK

As a pastry chef, you can work in a variety of establishments. Read about a few of them below. Think about which suit you best and why.

## RETAIL BAKERIES
Retail bakeries produce, package, and sell baked goods directly to customers.

## WHOLESALE BAKERIES
Wholesale bakeries are high-volume operations that produce baked goods to be sold in bulk to restaurants, grocery stores, and other establishments.

## RESTAURANTS
Some restaurants employ full- or part-time pastry chefs to create pastries and other baked goods for the menu.

## GROCERY STORE BAKERIES
Many grocery stores hire pastry chefs to produce fresh pastries and other baked goods to be sold at the store.

## HOME OR RENTED BAKERY
Some pastry chefs operate out of their home kitchens and sell goods to small shops or at farmers markets. Be sure to know your local laws before starting a business from your home. Alternatively, many pastry chefs rent commercial kitchen spaces.

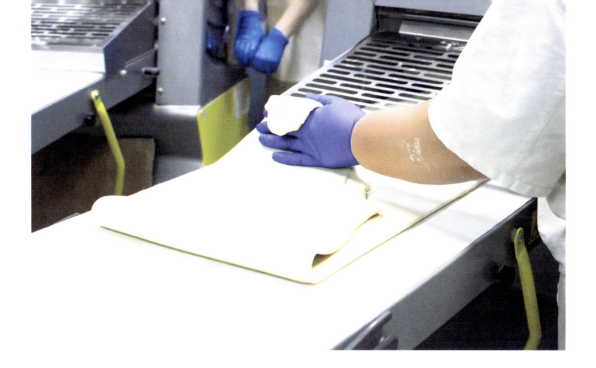

Depending on where you work, baking professionally can be drastically different from home baking. As you think about baking for a living, consider some of the tools, rules, and schedules of a professional baker.

## TOOLS

The tools of a professional pastry chef are built to produce large quantities of pastries and other baked goods. Industrial dough sheeters can rapidly roll out large pieces of dough. Commercial ovens and cooling racks hold dozens of pastries at a time. Commercial kitchens also order bulk ingredients, such as 50-pound (23 kg) bags of flour. Pastry chefs must be able to safely lift these heavy supplies.

## RULES

Pastry chefs must uphold cleanliness and food safety standards. These standards range from wearing a uniform and keeping hair pulled back to properly storing ingredients and thoroughly cleaning equipment after use. Pastry chefs must also follow rules to protect themselves and others from common kitchen hazards, such as hot pans and wet floors.

## SCHEDULES

Many pastry chefs start their work around 4 a.m. so their pastries are fresh and ready to sell a few hours later. They must be able to stay on their feet and maintain close attention to detail for many hours at a time. Retail bakeries and restaurants are especially busy during weekends, so most pastry chefs work at least one weekend day.

# DO WHAT YOU LOVE!

Being a pastry chef requires early hours, hard physical work, and attention to rules and details. These requirements can be difficult for home bakers to adjust to. But many pastry chefs find the rewards of their work outweigh the difficulties. These rewards include being creative, getting exercise, and learning new skills.

Maybe your goal is to manage a commercial kitchen. Maybe you have your sights set on owning a small pastry business. Or perhaps you are happy to keep making pastries as a hobby but not as a career. As long as you do what you love, you'll love what you do.

# GLOSSARY

**apprenticeship**—an arrangement in which a person learns a trade or a craft from a skilled worker.

**baklava**—a traditional Turkish, Greek, and Middle Eastern pastry made with phyllo dough, nuts, honey syrup, and spices.

**Crusades**—a series of Christian military expeditions, especially wars from the 1000s to the 1200s in which Christians sought to reclaim an area known as the Holy Land from Muslims.

**culinary**—having to do with the kitchen or cooking.

**edible**—safe to eat.

**enhance**—to increase or make better.

**establishment**—a place or organization where people do business.

**evaporate**—to change from a liquid into a vapor.

**fluted**—grooved or ridged.

**globalization**—the increase in the exchange of goods and knowledge around the world through trade and technology.

**gluten**—a protein found in many grains, such as wheat and barley.

**incorporate**—to include or work into.

**industrial**—of or having to do with factories and making things in large quantities. Industrialization is the transition to an industrial economy.

**innovation**—a new idea, method, or device.

**internship**—a program that allows a student or graduate to gain guided practical experience in a professional field.

**laminate**—to fold butter repeatedly into pastry dough to create layers.

**leavener**—a substance that creates air in a dough or batter to make it rise.

**overwork**—to knead or process dough too much, leading to tough, dense pastry or bread.

**retail**—related to the selling goods directly to customers.

**silicone**—a nontoxic substance made of silicon and oxygen atoms. It can take a rubber-like form, which is heat-resistant and used in many cooking and baking tools.

**soggy**—heavy and overly moist.

**technique**—a method or style in which something is done.

**tenderize**—to make softer or easier to cut and chew.

**wholesale**—relating to businesses that sell things in large amounts, often directly to other businesses.

# ONLINE RESOURCES

To learn more about careers as a pastry chef, please visit **abdobooklinks.com** or scan this QR code. These links are routinely monitored and updated to provide the most current information available.

# INDEX

aluminum foil, 31, 33, 55

baked goods, 7-8, 11, 20, 57-59
  baklava, 7
  bread, 7-8, 12
  cake, 7, 12
  cream puffs, 21, 24-25, 52-53, 55
  croissants, 7
  éclairs, 21, 24-25, 29, 49-53, 55
  galettes, 34-35
  pies, 7, 16-17, 21, 23, 27, 29, 31-34, 37, 39, 43, 54-55
  tarts, 7, 12, 17, 23, 37-41, 54-55
  turnovers, 12, 15, 21, 27, 43-46, 54-55
  twists, 46-47
bowls, 15, 23, 31-32, 34, 37-39, 43-44, 49-51

careers, 5, 57-59, 61
Carême, Marie-Antoine, 8
cheese, 34-35, 46
chilling, 17-18, 23, 32-34, 38-40, 44-46
chocolate, 13, 29, 34, 37-39, 46, 49-52
cinnamon, 11, 21, 31-32, 34, 46
color, 12, 18, 23, 33, 39, 45, 47, 51
cooling racks, 15, 31, 33, 37, 39, 43, 45, 49, 51, 59
cornstarch, 11, 49-50
Crusades, 8

dairy
  cream, 12, 15, 17, 37, 39, 41, 49, 51-54
  milk, 11-12, 18, 37, 39, 41, 49-50, 54
dough scrapers, 15, 23, 31-32, 37, 43

egg washes, 16, 18, 23, 31, 33, 35, 43, 45, 47
eggs, 11, 15-18, 20, 23, 25, 29, 31, 33, 35, 37-38, 40, 43, 45, 47, 49-51
Egypt, 7
electric mixers, 15, 41, 49, 51
Europe, 8

fats, 5, 7, 11-12, 18, 20-21, 23, 31-32, 37-40, 43-44, 49-50
flavor, 5, 7, 11, 13, 20, 27, 34, 37, 39-41, 49, 52, 54
flour, 7, 11-12, 17, 19, 21, 23, 25, 31-33, 37-38, 43-45, 49-50, 59
France, 8, 49
fruit, 11-12, 15, 21, 27, 31-34, 40-41, 43-46, 54-55

Greece, 7

icing, 12-13, 16, 29, 49, 51, 54-55

jam, 12, 40, 43, 45

knives, 21, 25, 29, 31-33, 37-39, 43-45, 47, 49, 51-52, 54

measurement, 27, 31-35, 37-38, 40-41, 43-47, 49-53

ovens, 7-8, 20-21, 25, 31, 33-34, 37, 39, 41, 43, 45, 49, 51, 59

pans, 15-17, 22-24, 31, 33-34, 37, 39-40, 43, 45, 47, 49-51, 55, 59
parchment paper, 16, 19, 24, 34, 37, 39-40, 43, 45, 47, 49, 51
pastry
  choux, 7, 12, 15, 21, 23-25, 29, 49-53, 55
  flaky, 5, 7-8, 11, 23, 31, 37, 43
  phyllo, 7
  puff, 7-8, 29, 43, 46
  shortcrust, 7, 23, 29, 37-39
pastry bags, 7, 16, 19, 24-25, 29, 49-53
pastry brushes, 16, 18, 23, 31, 35, 43, 45, 47
pastry cream, 11, 15, 17, 19, 29, 49-51, 55
pastry filling, 5, 11-13, 15-17, 19-21, 27, 31-35, 37, 39-41, 46, 52, 54-55
Persia, 8
pie weights, 17, 37, 39

piping, 7, 16, 19, 24-25, 29, 51-53
pizza cutters, 43, 45, 47
plastic wrap, 17, 31-32, 37-38, 43-44, 49-50, 55
preparation, 18-25, 27, 32, 34, 38, 44, 46, 50, 57

recipes
  apple pie, 31-33
  cheese & tomato galette, 34-35
  chocolate éclairs, 49-51
  chocolate tart, 37-39
  cream puffs, 52-53
  fruit turnovers, 43-45
  lemon tartlets, 40-41
  Nutella twists, 46-47
refrigerators, 17, 31-33, 37-39, 43-45, 49-50, 55
rolling pins, 7, 17-19, 23-24, 31, 33-34, 37-38, 43-46, 59
Rome, 7

safety, 5, 22, 25, 59
salt, 11, 13, 17, 29, 31-32, 34-35, 37-39, 43-44, 49-50, 54
spatulas, 17, 21, 37, 49
sugar, 8, 12-13, 17, 31-32, 37-39, 43-46, 49-50, 53-54

techniques, 5, 8, 18-21, 23-25, 27, 43, 57
technology, 8, 59
temperature, 11, 15-16, 20-21, 23, 25, 31, 33-34, 37-39, 41, 43, 45, 49-51, 53, 55, 59
texture, 5, 7-8, 11-13, 19-21, 23, 25, 29, 31, 37-39, 41, 43, 49, 50-51, 54
training, 5, 8, 57

vanilla extract, 13, 37, 39, 49-50, 53
vegetables, 34, 40

water, 7, 17-18, 20, 23, 25, 31-32, 37-38, 43-44, 49-51
whisks, 17-18, 23, 31-32, 37-39, 43-44, 49-50